present

DRIP FEED

by KAREN COGAN

Drip Feed was first performed on 1 August 2018
at Assembly as part of Edinburgh Festival Fringe.

DRIP FEED

Written and performed by

KAREN COGAN

Director	**Oonagh Murphy**
Set and Costume Designer	**Anna Reid**
Lighting Designer	**Jess Bernberg**
Sound Designer	**Frank Sweeney**
Stage Manager	**Jasmin Hay**
Producer	**Holly De Angelis**

BIOGRAPHIES

WRITER AND PERFORMER | KAREN COGAN

Karen trained as an actor at RADA. Her first play *The Half Of It* won the Stewart Parker Award in 2018 after a sold out run in Dublin. *The Half Of It* was nominated for five Fringe Awards and won the First Fortnight Award.

Karen's second play *Drip Feed* was shortlisted for the Verity Bargate Award. It reached the top six of 1,200 submissions. *Drip Feed* will have its world premiere with Soho Theatre and Fishamble in Edinburgh, Dublin and London. *Drip Feed* has been optioned and commissioned for television development by Witchery Pictures.

Karen has five original television shows in development with production companies.

She was shortlisted for the Red Planet Prize 2018 and the BBC Writers Room Drama Room 2019. She is RADA's submission for the Adopt A Playwright Award 2018 and was shortlisted for the award. Karen is the Hospital Club Theatre and Performance Emerging Creative 2018/19.Karen's writing has been supported by The Peggy Ramsay foundation. She was chosen to attend MAKE theatremakers residency in the Tyrone Guthrie Centre alongside international mentors and theatre artists.

Karen is one of the chosen playwrights for Fishamble's A Play For Ireland initiative 2018/19.

DIRECTOR | OONAGH MURPHY

Theatre credits include: *Shelter* (Druid Theatre Company, Galway International Arts Festival); *The Mouth of a Shark by THISISPOPBABY* (Where we live); *Tribes* (Gate Theatre, Dublin Theatre Festival) *Give Me Your Skin* (Battersea Arts Centre); *Mojo* (The Lir Dublin); *Foxy* (Project Arts Centre); *Be Infants In Evil* (Druid Theatre Company, Galway International Arts Festival); *Ribbons, Love in a Glass Jar* (the Peacock Stage at the Abbey Theatre 2012); *Taking Back Our Voices*, (commissioned by the Abbey Theatre 2012). Oonagh was Resident Assistant Director at the Donmar Warehouse in 2013, and Resident Assistant Director at the Abbey Theatre Dublin, 2011–2012.

SET AND COSTUME DESIGNER | ANNA REID

Training: Wimbledon College of Art. Designer credits include: *Dust, Fury, Brute* (Soho Theatre); *Schism* (Park Theatre); *Grotty* (The Bunker); *Rasheeda Speaking* (Trafalgar Studios); *Tiny Dynamite* (Old Red Lion); *Collective Rage, Dear Brutus, The Cardinal, School Play* (Southwark Playhouse); *The Kitchen Sink, Jumpers for Goalposts* (The Oldham Coliseum); *Sex Worker's Opera* (set only, national tour and Ovalhouse Theatre); *I'm Gonna Pray For You So Hard* (Finborough Theatre); *For Those Who Cry When They Hear The Foxes Scream* (Tristan Bates Theatre); *Dottir* (The Courtyard); *Dry Land* (Jermyn Street Theatre); *Arthur's World* (Bush Theatre); *Hippolytos* (Victoria and Albert Museum); *Hamlet* (The Riverside Studios).

LIGHTING DESIGNER | JESS BERNBERG

Training: Guildhall School of Music and Drama and the 2018 Laboratory Associate Lighting Designer at Nuffield Southampton Theatres. Design credits include: *A New and Better You, Buggy Baby* (The Yard); *The Marbleous Route Home* (Young Vic); *Reactor* (Arts Ed); *Dungeness, Love and Information* (Nuffield Southampton Theatres); *Devil with the Blue Dress, FCUK'D* (Off West End Award nomination) (The Bunker); *Split, WAYWARD* (Vaults); *The Blue Hour of Natalie Barney, The Dowager's Oyster, Youkali: The Pursuit of Happiness, The Selfish Giant* (Arcola Theatre); *The Death of Ivan Ilyich* (Merton Arts Space); *And the Rest of Me Floats* (Birmingham Rep); *And Here I Am* (UK tour. Co-Design with Andy Purves); *The Poetry We Make* (Vaults Festival/RADA/Rosemary Branch/Old Red Lion); *This is Matty, and He is Fucked* (Winemaker's Club); *Flux: Shadowlines* (King's Place); *SQUIRM* (King's Head/Theatre503/Bread & Roses Theatre/C Venues); *Glitter & Tears* (Bread & Roses Theatre/theSpace UK); *Balm in Gilead, The Same Deep Water As Me, August* (Guildhall). Assistant Lighting Designer: *A Streetcar Named Desire* (Nuffield Southampton Theatres); *A Tale of Two Cities* (Regent's Park Open Air Theatre); *Fox on the Fairway* (Queen's Theatre Hornchurch). Jess received the Association of Lighting Designer's Francis Reid Award in 2017.

SOUND DESIGNER | FRANK SWEENEY

Training: Masters in Music and Media Technologies at Trinity College Dublin and a Honours Degree in Visual Communications from the Dún Laoghaire Institute of Art, Design and Technology. Design credits include: *Heroin* (Spirit of the Fringe Winner); *The Game* (Dublin Theatre Festival); *The Shitstorm* (The Abbey) and *Not At Home* (Dublin Fringe, Winner of Best Production 2017). Assistant label manager at RVNG, Beats in Space and Software in New York 2014–15. Released and toured extensively as a DJ and producer over the past years under Frank B and Sias. Part of the Repeater collective, producing art and music in tandem physical formats, with complimentary events showcasing local artists.

Soho Theatre is London's most vibrant venue for new theatre, comedy and cabaret. We occupy a unique and vital place in the British cultural landscape. Our mission is to produce new work, discover and nurture new writers and artists, and target and develop new audiences. We work with artists in a variety of ways, from full producing of new plays, to co-producing new work, working with associate artists and presenting the best new emerging theatre companies that we can find.

We have numerous artists on attachment and under commission, including Soho Six and a thriving Young Company of writers and comedy groups. We read and see hundreds of scripts and shows a year.

'The place was buzzing, and there were queues all over the building as audiences waited to go into one or other of the venue's spaces... exuberant and clearly anticipating a good time.' Guardian.

We attract over 240,000 audience members a year at Soho Theatre, at festivals and through our national and international touring. We produced, co-produced or staged over 40 new plays in the last 12 months.

As an entrepreneurial charity and social enterprise, we have created an innovative and sustainable business model. We maximise value from Arts Council England and philanthropic funding, contributing more to government in tax and NI than we receive in public funding.

Registered Charity No: 267234

Soho Theatre, 21 Dean Street
London W1D 3NE
Admin 020 7287 5060
Box Office 020 7478 0100

OPPORTUNITIES FOR WRITERS AT SOHO THEATRE

We are looking for unique and unheard voices – from all backgrounds, attitudes and places.

We want to make things you've never seen before.

Alongside workshops, readings and notes sessions, there are several ways writers can connect with Soho Theatre. You can

- **enter** our prestigious biennial competition the **Verity Bargate Award** just as **Vicky Jones** did in 2013 with her Award-winning first play *The One*.

- **participate** in our nine month long **Writers' Labs programme**, where we will take you through a three-draft process.

- **submit your script** to submissions@sohotheatre.com where your play will go directly to our Artistic team

- **invite us** to see your show via coverage@sohotheatre.com

We consider every submission for production or any of the further development opportunities.

sohotheatre.com

Keep up to date:

sohotheatre.com/mailing-list
@sohotheatre all social media

About Fishamble: The New Play Company

Fishamble is an Olivier Award-winning, internationally acclaimed Irish theatre company, which discovers, develops and produces new work, across a range of scales. Fishamble is committed to touring throughout Ireland and internationally, and does so through partnerships and collaborations with a large network of venues, festivals and non-arts organisations.

Fishamble has toured its productions to audiences in Ireland as well as to England, Scotland, Wales, France, Germany, Iceland, Croatia, Belgium, Czech Republic, Switzerland, Bulgaria, Romania, Serbia, Turkey, Finland, USA, Canada, New Zealand and Australia.

Fishamble and Pat Kinevane won an Olivier Award for *Silent* in 2016, when it was presented at Soho Theatre. Other awards for Fishamble productions include Scotsman Fringe First, Herald Angel, Argus Angel, 1st Irish, The Stage, Adelaide Fringe Best Theatre, Dublin Fringe, EMA, In Dublin, Forbes' Best Theater, Stage Raw LA, and Irish Times Theatre awards, as well as Writers Guild of Ireland/ZeBBie and Stewart Parker Trust awards for many of its playwrights. Fishamble's living archive is in the National Library of Ireland.

Fishamble is at the heart of new writing for theatre in Ireland, not just through its productions, but through its extensive programme of Training, Development and Mentoring schemes. These currently include *A Play for Ireland,* the *New Play Clinic* and *Show in a Bag,* which is run in partnership with Dublin Fringe Festival and Irish Theatre Institute. Each year, Fishamble typically supports 60% of the writers of all new plays produced on the island of Ireland, approximately 55 plays per year.

'Fishamble puts electricity in the National grid of dreams'
Sebastian Barry

'a global brand with international theatrical presence' *Irish Times*

'forward-thinking Fishamble' *New York Times*

'excellent Fishamble... Ireland's terrific Fishamble' *Guardian*

Fishamble's recent and current productions include

Before by Pat Kinevane in association with the Stollers Network (2018)

Rathmines Road by Deirdre Kinahan in co-production with the Abbey (2018)

Drip Feed by Karen Cogan in co-production with Soho Theatre (2018)

GPO 1818 by Colin Murphy to mark the bicentenary of the GPO (2018)

Haughey|Gregory by Colin Murphy in the Abbey, Mountjoy Prison, Dáil Éireann and Croke Park (2018)

Maz & Bricks by Eva O'Connor on national and international tour (2017–18)

Forgotten, Silent and *Underneath* by Pat Kinevane (since 2007, 2011 and 2014, respectively – 2018) touring in Ireland, UK, Europe, US, Australia and New Zealand

On Blueberry Hill by Sebastian Barry on national and international tour (2017)

The Humours of Bandon by Margaret McAuliffe (2017–18) on national and international tour

Charolais by Noni Stapleton (2017) in New York

Inside the GPO by Colin Murphy (2016) performed in the GPO during Easter

Tiny Plays for Ireland and America by 26 writers (2016) at the Kennedy Center, Washington DC, and Irish Arts Center, New York, as part of *Ireland 100*

Mainstream by Rosaleen McDonagh (2016) in coproduction with Project Arts Centre

Invitation to a Journey by David Bolger, Deirdre Gribbin and Gavin Kostick (2016) in coproduction with CoisCeim, Crash Ensemble and Galway International Arts Festival

Little Thing, Big Thing by Donal O'Kelly (2014 - 16) touring in Ireland, UK, Europe, US and Australia

Swing by Steve Blount, Peter Daly, Gavin Kostick and Janet Moran (2014–16) touring in Ireland, UK, Europe, US, Australia and New Zealand

Spinning by Deirdre Kinahan (2014) at Dublin Theatre Festival

The Wheelchair on My Face by Sonya Kelly (2013–14) touring in Ireland, UK, Europe and US.

Fundraising Fellowship
Dublin

Business to Arts' New Stream programme in partnership
with Dublin City Council's *Dublin's Culture Connects*

Comhairle Cathrach
Bhaile Átha Cliath
Dublin City Council

Culture Ireland
Cultúr Éireann
Promoting Irish Arts in Britain

Acknowledgements

To Gabriel Pac, a human angel, without whom I'd be lost.

To my parents, Kay and Diarmuid Cogan, who give each other cards to mark their first date, after forty years of marriage. Without their sacrifices and wisdom, I wouldn't have even started down this path.

To my sister Michelle, who is the funniest, sharpest person I have ever met and whom I adore.

To Cathal Cleary for taking a full-hearted risk on *The Half Of It* and giving it clear direction in more ways than one.

Thank you to Steve Marmion and all at the Soho Theatre for changing the course of my career. To Jo Wiltshire, Lloyd Trott, Ed Kemp and all at the RADA Festival for a safe home for the beginning of both plays.

To the gifted actors and artists who helped birth the plays, particularly Naomi Cranston for her love and constant support. To Oonagh Murphy, a bright light and huge brain, Faoileann Cunningham, Grainne Keenan, Jessica Regan, Stephanie Racine and Eadaoin O'Donoghue, Tanya Ronder, Sam Taylor, John O'Dowd and Rosie Elnile.

To Anna and Kazimir and Grazia Pac for endless kindness. Ikenna Obiekwe at Independent, Deirdre O'Halloran, Mark Rylance, the Stewart Parker Trust and Lynne Parker, the London Irish Centre and the Hospital Club, all at Nick Hern Books, Fishamble, Mommo Theatre Co, Saileóg O'Halloran, Kelly Phelan, and Dublin Fringe Festival.

Thank you.

Karen Cogan

DRIP FEED

For Aisling O'Loughlin,
one of the best people I'll ever know.

Character

BRENDA, *a Cork woman, mid-thirties*

The action takes place in Cork City 1998. The setting should not be naturalistic.

The stage is clean, aside from some kind of structure, which could act as a bin, a bed, an escape, a stage, throughout the play.

Bold text in speech is used for emphasis.

Lines in italics are the words of others, as recalled by Brenda.

All characters should be embodied and lived by Brenda but should not be a performance, as much as a real attempt to make them live for the audience.

This text went to press before the end of rehearsals and so may differ slightly from the play as performed.

(BRENDA *faces the audience*.)

(*She lives the past, even in recollection.*)

Don't throw up Brenda, don't throw up now for fuck's sake.

(*To the audience*.) You know that feeling, when you are doing the absolute wrong thing but you keep going, like, as you go to do the thing your whole body says: Stop. Don't Do This.

I feel like that a lot. I can feel the Nos rise up in me but I'm so used to them now, I just let them wibble up and then ebb away and press on regardless.
Like now.

No. I'm just visiting.
She might want to see me. You don't know.
She might bloody be delighted to bollocking see me.
She wanted to see me when my head was between her legs.

Look at me Brenda, keep looking while you do it.

I thought I was going to get lockjaw trying to do the deed with my mouth and make sultry eyes at the same time, I looked demented. But it did the trick.
She was delighted with me then. So, maybe she'll welcome me with open arms now.

Come in, come in you gorgeous lunatic, what are you loitering out by my bins for? COME IN.
This woman? She's my hired help. Ignore her. Ignore her gleamy mirror hair. I've no interest. It's you. It's always been you Brenda.

No.
Okay.

She is Olivia, she is my girlfriend and I am hiding in her bin hut, balancing on a wheelie bin.

Who has a house for their bins?
But she was always immaculate; she would line up all her
toiletries in the bathroom in order of size and make sure that the
labels were facing the right way like an army of hygiene.

Frizzy hair Brenda, is a curse. You're so lucky with yours.

Her hair wasn't frizzy at all like, it was perfection but that's not
relevant.
What is relevant is her gorgeous attention to detail so... no
wonder her bins are housed.

Three different bins.
I can't work out what the square blue bin is for? Blue bin is a
bit far to go investigating and I'm already in very real danger of
my rain-soaked Converse sliding me off the one I'm on. But I
am very curious now to know what's in it.
Should never have started thinking so deeply about the blue bin
but here we are.
What is in it?? I thought we were only supposed to have one
bin. She's always extraordinary, always different from the rest
of us, a bit... better.

Fuck it. I have to know.
If she sees me I will...
(*She prepares to investigate, from her precarious position.*)
Okay. Be wide and stay low.

Crouching as small as I go, I slant my whole body to the right,
clinging onto the timbery wall for balance, the smells of my feet
and the bin rot creep deeper into my mouth but **but** I just
manage to grab the lid of the blue bin and launch it upwards. It
twhacks against the back of the bin house though and I teeter
and then bin totters underneath me.
I freeze. If one of them comes out to me I will be in Such Shit.
But.
Silence.
I'm okay I think.
And
The blue bin is full of paper, it's full of paper, oh.
But thick paper and kind of coloured canvases.

I pull one out, just about and hold it up to see, and it's her.
My girlfriend, a picture of her in thick colourful crayon strokes
and she is knotted laughing and she has no top on.
Laughing in the nude, all the colours blurred together and
beautiful, it is beautiful in fairness but
It's signed
Sam.
Sam.
Why are you painting my girlfriend naked Sam?
Why is Sam painting pictures of Olivia naked?

Fuck it. I'm taking it. She threw it away. Olivia is mine not
hers. Fuck it.
I shove the bright colours of her down the back of my pants and
edge out of their garden, swift and damp and careful.

Cork Streets

Walking through Cork now, streets on streets of badgering
memories
I used to have salami and cheese rolls with Olivia from that
Spar deli there, by the river.
Garlicky salami always defeated me, so I had to eat the whole
big slice at once instead of spreading the bites evenly through
the roll.
Olivia laughed at me and called me an idiot but she kissed my
nose, it's very intimate to kiss a nose. She's always kissing my
nose. Even though I look like Barbra Streisand without the
cheekbones.
Barbra Streisand is in a film right called *The Mirror Has Two
Faces* and she is ugly as anything in it and she falls in love with
this fella who only likes her for her personality because she is a
brilliant teacher. I am not a brilliant teacher.
I'm teaching no one nothing. I am on the part-time dole,
queueing on Tuesdays in a clump of people I know who don't
say hello to me.

Over Nano Nagle Bridge and down the Grand Parade. Nearing
the Coal Quay and my loins start to twist. My feet go shivery
and I walk slower, expecting her to pop out of Flat 19 over the
pub and go.

*What are you out here for? Come on in and we'll bunker down
out of this rain? I got a new Angelina Jolie DVD and a pizza.*

I've always wanted to see her more often than she wanted to
see me.
Give me time to miss you.
But the feeling of her is kind of insidious. Like, my ears miss
her. It's not all vaginas.
It's the sad eyes she makes when she's half-asleep and the way
she cocks her head to the side like a Fraggle. It's the anxiety,
like the constant crushing in my chest, the sense of falling and
of my mind resetting and forgetting… things.
And her. The artist. Sam. Cunt

Sam is.
Sam is English.
And a lovely painter apparently, which is, y'know…
They could be naked and having the craic together right now for
all I know: laughing or riding I don't know which is worse.
Oh God, the notion of them sitting in silky pyjamas, drinking
something, tea or beer with their legs interlaced like an ad for
SuperValu, y'know where there are kids and puppies and
gorgeous couples, not gay couples obviously. You'd never see
gay couples in an ad for picking up bread in the morning. But, if
you did.

I shove the painting further down the back of my jeans as it
starts to ride up and out attempting an escape. I fold it in four
and shove it between the waistband of my knickers and my skin
and tie my belt tight as it goes.

What are you doing there Brenda girl. Are ya alright like?

I'm grand John, thanks.

Fucking John Morley, in his cream tracksuit staring at me like I'm a zoo monkey.

Grand altogether. Just when I saw you rabitting around in your trousers there I thought you might be having a problem. But you're definitely grand are ya? Good. Listen, I saw your sister on Tuesday and I said to her and I'll say the same to you now – Listen John, mind yourself. I'm up the walls. See ya.

And onwards.

John Morley's one of the lads from around who is obsessed with me going out with girls; the questions he asks me while he collects white bits in the corners of his mouth.

Where's your lovely lady tonight? Not with you? I thought ye were joined at the hip no? Linking arms around town. Like sisters. Except there's one important difference isn't there ha? Ho ho yes there is.
And tell me this, will ye be life partners now? Will ye live together as if yer a married couple?
Yer comforting to each other are ye?
Must be good to share dresses and and and and moisturiser with each other.
Do ye not miss men?
Who fixes things when they break Brenda?
What is it about men you don't like?
Is it the hairiness?
We're hairy alright in fairness.
Although women can be hairy.
But ye don't seem that hairy.
But who knows ha?
Who knows what's beneath the sheets as they say?
Ha?
What lies beneath like.
Ye could be very hairy.
Feminists I suppose.
Girl power gone mad ha?
Fair play to ye.

He should have paid us for his lesbian lessons. But John Morley is the least of my worries in Cork. Olivia is fierce dramatic looking, long mad curly hair in about twenty-seven different shades of brown and black and huge dark eyes and we get a lot of comments on the streets. Fellas hanging out of vans and cars and windows. Just letting us know they can see us like.

Alright ladies can I get in between ye? How are ye girls? Heading home for some fun? I know what yer up to. Room for one more? Can I watch? Can we watch? Can we film it? Oh to be a fly on the wall? What I wouldn't give boys.

But me and her rose miles above everyone.

Even when the skinny man in the saggy jeans spat in my face. He smelt like last week's tobacco and I could see his pores for a split second as he leaned in to our faces. We were close together on Popes Quay, bent laughing at something Olivia had said, I can't remember what but... she's very funny. And I could see the crinkles by her eyes and I thought why would anyone fight the seven signs of ageing if they're this divine?

Then.
DYKES. And spat. I sniffed his spit as I wiped it away, couldn't help it. It was almost yellow, that's not right. He'd be better off down the doctor's like.
Olivia didn't do anything except hold my hand tighter and take me for a brandy in Loafers pub.

We didn't tell anyone in Loafers; not that there was many in there at half-four on a Wednesday. Just skinny Finbarr on his usual stool, smoking and welcoming us into the smell of last night's farts and Tanora underfoot and beer taps that always needed changing. Lovely Loafers. A welcome escape from comments and spit.
This one, Katie Watkins right, used to do maudlin lesbian poetry readings in there every Monday night and me and Olivia were obsessed with them. Our favourite was the one that started: *I want to wear you on my fist like a shield.*

We used to say it to each other instead of I love you.

Olivia?
Yeah?
I want to wear you on my fist like a shield
Oh thanks very much. I want to wear you on my fist like a shield too Brenda.

(*Fondly.*) Loafers. Simply Red and Celine Dion or 'Barbie Girl' blasting out from Red FM. I'm tempted to cross over the bridge and pop in now. Be nice to sit under the square telly that's always showing the news on a loop, Good Friday agreement and all that craic. Oddly calming like.
Only, they've started doing lunches. Lunches – (*Tuts*.) And the smell of the soup mingling with the pub stink is noxious.
And people stare at you if you go in on your own. It's not the same really.
Notions.

Onto North Main Street, it's all foreign shops now. Foreign.
Ya, I suppose, 'cause they didn't grow up here. They didn't live in tiny two-up two-downs with aggressive, pretend plants in the living room and glossy wallpaper masquerading as expensive.

Upwardly mobile: my sister Rita and my mam Orla. Upwardly mobile sums them up alright.

What does she have now? Where did she get the money for that? That's fake I'm sure, there's no way she can afford that. State of your wan, who does she think she is, did you see what Aisling Sullivan's daughter was wearing in the Echo *last night? Why is she always on the* Echo? *Why do you never get in the* Echo? *What bars do you be going to, to say that you never see the* Echo *photographer? Maybe if you dolled yourself up a small bit more, you've nice breasts, shove them up and hide that stomach and just put yourself out there. I'm not trying to be funny Brenda girl but time is ticking.*

And then she died. My mam. Dead mam, very sudden; her heart went.
She had a chocolate éclair three times a day every day and had done since she was a waitress in in her twenties. Thirty-odd years of three éclairs a day, that must be… like… hundreds of thousands of éclairs. No wonder her heart gave in.

And after she was in the ground: sisters were doing it for
themselves in the two-up two-down. Rita and me.
My sister is a bulldog in white jeans but beautiful eyes, green
and kind. We'd a lovely time, chatting and thick sandwiches
with Utterly Butterly and hunks of cheese. And beers from
Galvin's, dancing to 96 FM in the kitchen.
Me and Rita had a good thing going until the Gay Epiphany.

I thought she was going to **melt** into the ground when she
finally caught me with Olivia.

Me and Liv had had daytime white wine down the alley by The
Roundy House pub the day we got caught. A bottle each,
downed and then sexy squabbling through the streets, in a
different time zone to everyone else, like a French couple.
I was trying to apologise for whatever I'd said wrong to Olivia
so I caught up with her on the Coal Quay and grabbed her waist
and then her hands and I kissed her hard on the mouth and from
behind her head

Rita.

White face frozen, like that *Scream* painting.
Hissing.

Get. Up. Home

I didn't have the bravery to say no.

So home to
Lesbian this, disgrace that.

I love her Rita. I'm just gay. That's all.

Gay? Gaaayyyyy?

You're about as gay as the dog.

*Why do you always have to be different? What am I supposed to
tell the girls? Jesus Christ, who else saw ye mauling each
other? Bold as brass in the middle of the day! Do you actually
not think about anyone except yourself?*
I can't.
No.

Get out Brenda.
I'm sorry.
You're not welcome. Get Out.

I begged her. To let me stay in the house.
Mortified in hindsight. But. No-go.
I stayed on a bench in Fitzgerald's Park for two nights with the winos 'cause Olivia had to go away working in England.

But then: Veronica, my ferocious best friend rescued me. She bumped into me looking like a junkie, stringy hair dripping into my eyes from the constant constant rain, even in June. Pissing Ireland.

She screamed at me from across the bridge on Sullivan's Quay that night.
Brenda! Brenda!
What are you wandering round in the lashing rain for you gobshite. BRENDA! Come up to my place.

Veronica installed me on the couch in her tiny one -bed flat, then she put me on the back of her bike and drove us over to my mam's house, eh Rita's house and stood outside, looking like a policewoman from a porn film in tight jeans and a leather shirt.

Go in and get your stuff and I'll take you back to ours.

I'll just see if she's calmed down...

No. Go in get a bag and leave.

Skulking around the bedroom shoving random bits of underwear and letters into a rucksack and Rita walked in so we exchanged shit pleasantries and it was awful, until I looked up and Veronica was standing over us with her hand outstretched.

Give me the bag and get on the bike.

Just a second Veronica.

Get on the bike Brenda. She doesn't deserve your company.

Ah now.

She doesn't deserve your fucking company. Outside.

Like a dykey Indiana Jones.
Rita didn't know whether to kiss her or call a priest.
Veronica is so unapologetically gay. She is gay out the door, gay all day. Never let a man go near her.

We sat in her flat later on, looking down at Cork, drinking powdery hot chocolate and Baileys and she exploded in a rage.

How dare she judge you because of who you kiss, how dare she like! It's her loss, you're a champion and she's a fucking amoeba.

I see her in town all the time now of course, Rita, officious in leggings. Storming down Patrick Street jeans burrowing into her, with a Nike bag across her body and Dunnes Stores groceries failing to weigh her down. I have to launch myself into doorways and round corners to avoid her.
I veer parallel to Patrick Street now, as I head towards the flat and stay away from her well-worn patterns round town.

I'm getting my period I think.
My stomach has gone grippy and I don't want to bleed on the painting in my knickers so I readjust it and tackle the massive hill to Veronica's flat, home like.

Veronica's House

I peel my jeans off the second I get into the house and leave them on Veronica's floor like I'd dissolved. The painting falls out, on the ground, hot and crumply.
A bit of Blu Tack and it's up on the wall of Veronica's room with a desk lamp trained on it so I can see it in its full glory. She looks incredible. I can almost, almost forget who painted it. It's actually comforting to lie underneath the shape of her.

An hour later and I bolt up, crampy and late for work. Christ. The softness of Veronica's bed made a change from my timber sofa but now I'm late.

I roll off Veronica's drooly pillow and check I haven't stained the mattress with my now quite aggressive period. There's a burgundy spot alright, I'll sort it out later. She won't mind. She won't know anyway.

Work, a Café Called 'Café'

Can I help you? (*Listens*.)
No that doesn't come with peas. They're one pound extra.
(*Listens*.)
Okay, well how about you shit the shit off and buy your own tin of peas so.

Fucking work. Tiny café, smells of ass. No matter how much we bleach it, deep dirt.

We sell sandwiches and cakes with bright-pink icing, the kind of colour that does not occur in nature and Malcom my boss is a bit of a downer like.

It's all a bit
Tut, ah sure.
His son Martin fell into the river and died after he took seven Es and Malcom makes everything about him. He references him in every second sentence and it is draining.

Egg mayonnaise is it?
Oh Martin's favourite, well he preferred egg mayonnaise and ham, but still.
He loved sandwiches.
You could offer him a roast dinner and he'd take a sandwich over it any day.
Sandwich mad
He's Gone now o' course.
But shur look.

It's not worth the seven pounds an hour like but I have to live.

And the day presses on with a constant stream of gobshites looking for chocolate slices and chips and beans and stew, God help them, the stew is violent.

Still have six hours to go. Dragging crumbs around tables and Olivia. Olivia haunting me.
I just want to cradle her velvety neck and say:
If something about me is not good enough for you, I will change it. If it is the nose I will break it and get a man to rebuild it. If it is the flab I will do the cabbage-soup diet and properly this time, better than the time you caught me eating a whole sliced pan with jam on day two.
Is it 'cause I don't ever watch the news?
God it's agony.

Phone is going and going.
Constant ringing.
Malcom the PHONE!
Whenever I answer it, he acts affronted as if I'm stealing his personal business.

Excuse me girl I'll answer me own phone if you don't mind!
BUT:
BRENDA!
Phone for you.

Oh.
I pick it up
And I hear her, exhaling smoke and coughing like an exhaust pipe.
Oh my God.
Veronica?

I'm out Brenda. I'm up home.

And... are you better?

I'm great girl, out the other side finally.
Come on home. I've a bottle of vodka.

YESSSSSS!
My pal is back.

Malcom. I'm dying. Malcom I'm very faint. I'm dying like. I'll
have to go rest. Sorry Malcom.
Malcom you'll be grand. I'll see ya Monday Malcom.

Are you off your actual game girl? It's the teatime rush.

Malcom I've my PERIOD. I'm pumping blood like. Clots
Malcom.

*(Flustered.) Oh, well. Right. Okay. Sure look. I dunno. Right.
Well.*

Out of there and up to her. Panting at the hilltop but Cork is
laying out, shimmering a bit below, goldfish on the left and
river in front. Want to bask in it but can't wait to clap eyes on
Veronica back in residence.

Veronica won't know herself, back home in our little flat. It'll
be gorgeous to have her head back around the place. Her skin is
like a pearl or, or a, a llama's eye; llamas' eyes are really brown
and kind aren't they and you kinda want to lay down in them.
That doesn't make sense but do you know what I mean? She's
like a llama... a gorgeous woman llama, muscular like.
Like Sonia O'Sullivan, if Sonia O'Sullivan was more of a ride.
No judgement Sonia you seem... nice enough.
And very fast obviously
A bit stern. But sure you're busy.
Veronica is kind of lithe and like nothing seems like too much
bother for her body y'know? Like she bends in funny directions
when there's no need; her elbow could get your tea off the shelf
for you, ya know?
Look, she's bendy.
And funny.

And
We kissed when we were eighteen.
It seemed like the only thing to do.
I'd been riding my toy elephant for two years and I was getting
friction burns.
I'd all sort of fantasies when I was with him and I don't think
they were even primarily sexual but more like fantasies of
running for the fucking hills. And my groin seemed to be the

best thing to start moving instead of my legs
So as was my nightly routine, I started grinding up on my toy
elephant Bono. He's no relation to actual Bono, God forbid.
Actual Bono is like a leg of pork in a jacket.
Veronica was staying over and she heard me even though I was
only doing it subtly that night and she goes

What are you doing? Are you riding your elephant?

I was so mortified I thought I'd disintegrate.

Wwhaaaattttttt?
No!
Am I whatttt?? You're a psycho.

Are you sleeping with Bono Brenda?

Nooooooooooooo
I am not
What?

*Ah Jesus Brenda how long has this been going on? Are you that
frustrated?*

(*Pause.*)

Yes

Me too

And then we lay there for a while until she hooted out into the
darkness

Will we kiss?

And I went

Em...

Yeah. Go on

And I got into her shiny green sleeping bag and we'd to unzip it
and let out all the warmth. It was Baltic and I edged in and we
kissed a bit.
But
It was like rubbing two shins together, closed reluctant flat
mouths; like licking sandpaper.

But it was both our first time kissing a girl instead of wanging
on about it or writing winding diary entries and bad poems
about it.
A safe start to the gayness.
We bent ourselves double mocking each other's mouths
afterwards 'til we fell asleep on the floor under the bag with
with our arms knotted up.
So we wouldn't get weird with each other in front of Rita the
next day.
We never ever did it again but we kind of never let go of each
other's arms either.

Veronica's House

She hasn't been 'well in herself'. But…
I tried to go once a week to see her but. It's tough.
God the state of that place they had her in. No one chats.
The lithium had her mellowed but tears came out of her eyes
constantly so you're not sure when she's crying and when it's
just water.

In the trunk by her bed, there's hundreds of small teddy bears
from when we went round to every charity shop in Cork buying
all the teddies.

We can't leave them Brenda, they've soulful eyes.

And she dragged me around for three days until we had bought
every teddy bear in Cork and spent every penny of both of our
doles. We lived on stale corn flakes and sweetcorn from a tin for
seven days.

I thought I should bring her up a few of the teddies actually.
The only thing is, the sight of them would have reminded her of
all the new ones that would have been donated since she got put
up above and she'd have had me all over Cork. So I didn't.
One time we went to Midleton on the bus because she
overheard an aul wan saying 'there are grand second-hand

shops below in Midleton'. We didn't get back 'til all hours 'cause we had to sit in rush-hour traffic.

We had teddies and dolls and butterfly toys, fat snails and smiling cows and even a furry penis left over from a hen night, falling out of our every crevice and people thought we were absolutely off our heads. Well, one of us was I suppose.

I don't think of her as sick. I just think of her as my best friend. Sick yeah but brilliant too. They're not mutually exclusive. I only learnt what that meant recently. So like okay, mutually exclusive. It's that two things can be the same and still not... .no. It means that one thing is not necessarily. No, so like if I say to you: I am living up in Sunday's Well but I also... No. FUCK. Okay maybe I need to work on that a small bit more.

And **here she is**, throwing open our yellow door, and her face is shiny and she's herself again. Like she climbed back into her own body and it is actually her looking through her eyes instead of some dreadful stranger.

Who are we meeting Veronica?

Everyone! It's Saturday night like.

And she downs another tumbler of vodka 7 Up.

We sit in the empty bath holding each other's knees. That's our favourite spot, with the bath curtain closed and the lights off.

It's better now is it? Your... mind like?

Much better dote.

Sorry I didn't come up to see you more. I should have brought you a bear.

Ah it was fucking depressing. Let's have another one.

And the two of us dance to the Indigo Girls holding hands and twirling, we're nothing if not clichéd but I fucking love the Indigo Girls. Their voices harmonising together, they make an unbelievable sound and we sing and pound our feet in every room of the flat.

And we go to Loafers first for pints, then The Other Place for shots and a dance downstairs and then to Sir Henry's 'cause it's

Saturday and there is **nowhere on this wide earth** like Henry's on a Saturday night

Even Nirvana played here a few years ago
So.
Sir Laurent Garnier says Henry's is the best crowd he ever played to in all his live long days including New York
So.
Carl Cox had to be physically dragged away from the decks like.

Sir Henry's Nightclub

Not a hundred per cent sure where everyone is exactly.
But I know I am delighted.
My jeans are soaking up a lot of vodka and mulch and possibly puke from the floor but I just roll them up to my thighs and I'm grand.
I can't see that well and the wine is making all my aches and pains fuck off tiny shots of green Apple Sourz on offer ten for a fiver so I buy another round and keep adding them to the swirling mixture in my gut I feel very healthy and free
Tomorrow will be different yes but Tomorrow is not here
Tomorrow didn't come out for a drink **I did**. Now. With my pals with my pals Veronica and Annie and Jean and Liz and and other good women. They are good people. They are different and ferocious and Jean is kind of sexy sometimes but no one no one holds a candle to Olivia.
To my girlfriend
My girlfriend is in event planning she plans huuuge events the whole events from start to finish and people cannot get over her like people think she is unreal altogether and they can't believe she's Irish 'cause she's better than all the English girls at it she used live in England yeah, London yeah Camden but now she's back it was vury hard Long distance ya Fierce strain on the two of us but she's back now reunited and it feels so good y'know?
Do you want a shot? Have a shot? Get her a shot. Have a shot.

You're only young once.

Moving on, onwards and dancing in the back bar to Stevie G doing 'No Diggity' and over there Tori Amos and Larry Levan and Snoop Dogg and Frankie Knuckles and hardcore something and different Tunes and the beats of them all, the beats, clashing from all of the rooms of the club, y'know they should sound bad all mixing together but it sounds amazing it sounds like someone should record the mix of them and make it into its own song That's a good idea Brenda I should tell someone Beautiful thick sound.

I have a pint of Heineken that a man put a shot of tequila into I told him to piss off but I grabbed it from him anyway and the taste is grand Mingling with all of the strangers but no one is reeeally a stranger in Henry's I see Sarah Murphy's brother Michael chatting to Laura Hanley from my class

Alright Laura

Dull as a wall that one

And Jessica Bradley is grinding herself up on…

Veronica

Jesus

Jessica Bradley's married like.

Veronica looks langers but shag it She deserves it She deserves a bit of a celebrate after everything she's been through

I'm proud of her I'm proud of Cork I'm proud of everyone

I climb up on a round table with graffiti all over it and I scream to the crowds:

UP CORK

GO ON CORK

LET'S FUCKING DANCE LADSSSSSS

And a few scream back and a few don't but that's grand

It's all grand and I'm floating on them then everyone is lifting me up with their words

I love your top girl
You look fierce well
What are you up to

Olivia

Olivia is up

Olivia is what I'm up to
Look at her
Isn't she divine
Me and my girlfriend Olivia are
Divine like
Me and Olivia my girlfriend are going to Mauritius
Me and my girlfriend are actually thinking about New York in
the spring
As a couple
My girlfriend
Olivia
Divine
Events
Girl
Woman
Olivia
Beautiful
Look at her
Woman
Girl
Friend
Partner
Picture
Look at her
And I
Not sure
Exactly
Where
How come?
Four
Paracetamol
Slamming
Head
Shots
Headache and thump
Small
Rest
Lie down
Cold tile

Toilet
Lovely
And
Maybe
Tomorrow
Will be

Kinder.

(*Pause*.)

Death.
Murder.
I am dying.
My gums are thirsty and my tongue is a husk.
Dust ball lodged in my throat making me gawk.
Vomit escapes out of me before I have a second to think about
where to aim it.
Clean it later.
Vommy chin though.
And the smell makes me go again.
This is a bad one.
I'll drag myself to the shower in a minute.
I just can't warm up.
VERONICA CLOSE THE WINDOW
Unstick my eyes from the tarry sleep to see how bad things are
this time.
My lips are old balloons and I'm pretty sure I'm cut but I can't
face looking. Not Yet.

(*Abrupt terrified pause*.)

Why am I outside?

FUUUCCCCKKKKKKKKK!

I am outside Olivia's house, again.
But not in the bin hut today.
At her front door.
Lying on the step.
No wonder my side is killing me.

Quiet my breathing.
I can't actually cope with this.
Sssh.
Fuck.
Drag my carcass up
Off a mat that says Welcome,
Doubt it.
Then.

Madam
Madam can you come away from the door please

Shiny black shoes and a cheap navy trouser.

Can only be

I'm Garda Flynn, from Sunday's Well Station.
There's been a complaint of disturbance.
Is this your house?

It's
It's my girlfriend's house.

And
The lie comes easy.
Girlfriend
Never trained my mouth to stop saying it.
She's not my girlfriend
People must think I'm loopy.
A long line of all the faces I've said it to over the years…
How many of them knew?
That we weren't long-distancing, she was just distancing
Herself
As far away as possible from me
And now

How am I here?
I've done a pool of boozy puke on her prickly welcome mat.
My left breast is flopping out of my bra in a bid for freedom and
I threw my holdy-in knickers in a bin somewhere last night so
I'm fecking free-bleeding and my mouth is thumping with pain.
And I am about to come face to face with her, for the first time in

Three Years
With
My girlfriend
My Ex-Girlfriend.
Gard knocks again
And she unhooks a bolt from inside. Keeping intruders away.
And there is the shadow of her behind the door.
God, I even fancy the outline of her.
But.
It's not her.
That's not Olivia.
And.
Her voice, all English and gentler than I imagined.

Garda Flynn goes:
Is this your girlfriend?
She makes a noise

No.
She says.

I can't look at her. I look at my knees, bleeding.
Brilliant.

Brenda? It's Brenda is it?

My name sounds like a potato in her accent.
Pathetic.

Hello it's Sadie is it?

I attempt.

It's Sam actually.

Whatever

I'm sorry. I had no choice but to call someone this time. You turned up at half-six in the morning screaming and singing Joni Mitchell songs and throwing your shoes at our window.

I feel my bare feet on the mat and know she's right.

BUT. Where's Olivia?
Why didn't she come to the door herself?

I want to ask your one but my mouth is glued shut with mortification.

Gard is getting bored of this Sunday-morning domestic and wants to go for a cup of tea.
Sam is not impressed but Olivia is not coming to the door. Even now and I suddenly know it's because

Olivia did not want her to call the Gards!

Pounding shuffles to the back of my head to make way for elation, for the joy of Hope. The joy of her. The realisation that Olivia did not want me to get into any trouble. Because She sees me. She knows me.
Maybe she quite liked the idea of me close by while she slept. Because.
She still cares about me.

I won't be any more trouble. I apologise Garda
I apologise Sadi... Sam. Honestly.

And.

Cork Streets

Free.
Of her, venomous manipulative stick of an English bitch, trying to convince Olivia to distance herself from me, calling the law. Because I just what? Turned up?
Turning up is not actually a crime in this country Sadie so tell Tony Blair or someone to send a plane for you and just fuck off.

As I reach the Opera House it becomes clear that the elated adrenaline was just a stand in for the absolute Horrors that are starting to seep into me.

Nasty old flashbacks of Olivia as I cross into town, past Supermac's.
Memories of the day she left me in there with curry chips going

soggy from my tears.
Her words from that day are coming in and into my skull.

Telly and Drinking. Telly, drinking. Stagnant. Expanding into your own sofa.
Don't you want to do better than this? Is this it for you? There's a whole world out there Brenda.

I am going. You know I'm going to travel around France Olivia. I told you. I'm going to pick grapes and go to Paris and… I'm looking into it.

When. When are you going to France? You've been looking into it for two years. You won't cross the river to try a new sandwich place Brenda. You cancel your dole appointments so you can watch telly for longer. You're not going anywhere. France.
I'll come back in a few years and you'll still be going to the same pubs with Veronica, laughing about that one time you threw a pencil parer at Mrs Sweeney at the blackboard and because her hair was so big she didn't feel it.

It was **Mr** Sweeney actually. That's the whole point of the story. He didn't feel it 'cause his hair was so massive –

Jesus Christ. Who cares? You're part of the Cork furniture and that's… it.

Stop.

Stabby pains in my ears and very badly needing a loo.

The Gingerbread House Café

I dive into The Gingerbread House and lock myself in the big loo in the back staircase. There is a smell of coleslaw and burnt toast and appalling coffee and it sneaks up my nostrils and my stomach starts to go again.
Jesus, what did I eat?
Vaguest recollection of a stale breakfast roll.

Centra. Yeah.

I throw up, black pudding and old egg, barely digested.

That roll would have been sitting under the heat lamps since half-seven in the morning. They shouldn't have sold that to me at all. Not on.

I gawk and gawk and gawk again until I can gawk no more.

There's a reflection of me watching me. She's in the full-length mirror next to the toilet. Who wants to watch themselves going?

Sitting on the loo and I'm staring at the mess in the mirror. I'm like a drunk Michael Jackson song.

Mouth looks worse than I thought, slit lips and – (*Notices.*) chipped tooth. Balls

Flab plopping over the waist of my low-slung jeans with the chain on the pocket. 'Makes me look edgy,' I thought when I bought it in Paul Street Shopping Centre but now it just looks embarrassing.

I'm thirty-four.

I thought that by now I'd… NO! No.

I consider staying on the cistern and hoping I eventually drown in it but…

ANYWAY! Onwards and upwards.

I skulk out of the café avoiding the aul wans having midday ham sandwiches. They stare but I duck out the side door and down towards Patrick Street.

Veronica must be dying if I'm this bad; she was annihilated by half-seven. She didn't know her name at 3 a.m. when we danced to 'Unfinished Sympathy' in a mad clump of people. It's always 'Unfinished Sympathy' by Massive Attack at the end of the night in Henry's. Everyone fucked and best friends with everyone.

Poor thing. I'll bring her a Lucozade in a while. Lucozade and a bag of Tayto will sort her out.

Not yet though.

She's like a poltergeist with a hangover, weeping and scratching or worse; catatonic, staring at home-improvement programmes for hours.

I'll go up to her shortly.

On Oliver Plunkett Street I realise I stink, pungent. And I badly
need a tampon now.
I'm digging in my deep pockets for one, among hard tissue
paper and chewing gums and hair clips when I can just feel her,
in front of me, appalled.

Rita.

Normally I'd never come down Oliver Plunkett on a Sunday
'cause I know Rita goes for a cooked breakfast in Scotts Bar
with her horrible friends.
Judgey girls with spite and cheap blusher coming out of their
temples.

*Hi Brenda, how are ya keeping? You're looking lovely in your…
big shirt aren't ya?*

I'm in one of my several 'No-Go Rita' zones but I'm not thinking
straight 'cause of the booze and the pain in my face and the clots
plopping out of me and I fucked up and here she is.
She takes me in and I see a glimmer of soft in her.

Jesus Brenda.
Are you alright?
Do you know you're bleeding down your top?

My mouth is filling with blood. I've split it afresh, trying to
smile at Rita.
She reaches for my hand and her eyes are filling up.
Mother of Christ, I've never seen her like this. She didn't cry at
our mam's funeral. I was like a hose.

I don't know what to say to her. I love her cross face but I am
dripping old blood out of two places and my gut tells me I
should leave her alone before anyone she knows sees us
together and she bristles and walks away from me.

So I let go of her hand and walk past her down towards Grand
Parade.
I can feel her standing behind me, calling me back through
gritted teeth, but I keep moving, stomach empty and body
lagging until I settle in the record section at the back of Cork
City Library.

I put George Michael on the listening station and settle into a
big chair, the red wool on it is scratchy but otherwise it's womb
comfortable.
I have to picture Olivia next to me to go to sleep. My head is
swimming and soon I'm out for the count.

Tribes won't let me in 'cause of my 'attire'. Tribes like.
It's a cafe for fifteen-year-olds to shift each other on sofas, with
security outside in the middle of the day.
I said to your man on the door:
Oh God you'd wanna have a look in the mirror love. You're a
pretend bouncer at a sandwich shop!
I turn the corner fast in case he comes after me.

The Oval isn't open for some reason and I can't go into the
Spailpín Fánach because my uncle drinks there.

I'd still be safe in the library if it wasn't for dopy Paudie
standing over me. I woke up and he was shuffling and humming
with both of his hands deep in his pockets. He has a simple
enough face but there's something very creepy about his crotch.
So I bolted.
I'm sitting on the footpath outside the Beamish Brewery and
tears are pooling on my collarbone and if anyone sees me I will
actually liquidise and flow down the drain like.

I don't know where to go. I want to kidnap Sam or Sadie or
whatever and dump her in the sea so I can lay with Olivia and
fiddle with her thumb and talk about how clouds happen.

I need a sausage sandwich with ketchup and mayonnaise mixed
together and a slice of cheese on top. I need a cup of tea. With
my sister.
I want my sister and the way she used to be.
I want the comfort of her, the warmth of pyjamas and the
Superser in the kitchen and the kettle on constant boil for cup
after cup until we feel better. Tiny telly on the countertop and
we'll watch something and not say anything.

She looked pure upset on the street when I walked away.

Maybe she was about to invite me up home.
Maybe…
(*A decision.*)
Okay.

Rita's House

I linger at the corner of the estate for as long as I dare.
Rain is spitting at me so I suck in my fear and approach.
Outside her door and I'm doing deep breathing. Can't knock.
Jacqueline next door is staring at me through her curtains but
I can't knock. Can't bring myself to.

*Are you alright Brenda love? She's inside alright. Just knock on
the door.*

I know how to get in Jacqueline. Thanks.

You're in an awful state aren't ya girl. What happened ya?

Fucking Jacqueline.

I pound on the door and dash to the side window and pound that
too to escape Jacqueline's chin hairs and nosiness.

And there she is. Rita.
A bit puffy-looking, holding a washing-up sponge.

Come in.

You sure?

Just come in love.

Relief.

Strong tea and three Kimberley biscuits and it smells like Fairy
Liquid and my mam and I am breathing a bit freer.
I stare at Rita's face 'cause she's looking out the window at
Jacqueline's hateful cat bothering a brown bird. This is the
closest I've been to her in a long while and she has some new

lines around her mouth and her lipstick is bleeding into them in pink streams.

Do you want more tea?

Can I make it?

Grand

We're face to face then and I smile a bit at her so she knows I still think she looks nice.

I'm worried Brenda.
Are you on drugs? Are you in trouble with the law? Are you...
a prostitute?

Rita please

Why are you bleeding? Who saw you in town like that?
Do you need to go talk to someone? Something isn't right with
you.
What are you doing for work? When did you last visit Mam's
grave?
Who knows about the gayness? We need to do something about
you.

Endless and my stomach is in my shoes and my breath bellows back up into my chest.

I'm focusing on the air freshener and the spotless empty oven and the six-pack of beans on the floor, not put away yet after the big shop. That's a lot of beans for one woman living alone. All this space and I'll be back on the old couch under the window now Veronica is home.
Couldn't she just get over it?

I'm just gay get over it.

And I feel my head rising up from the beans to face my sister. And I say:

I'm actually leaving.

What?

I'm Emigrating.

It's not emigrating any more Brenda. There's no coffin-ships involved.

I'm **moving** then. I'm moving to France. I leave this evening.

France?

Paris actually.

Paris?

Yes Paris.

What are you going to do in Paris?

I'm not sure Rita but I'll bloody be in Paris.

Thats a big expensive city dote. You get lost in Clonakilty.

Just… PARIS RITA.
Bye-bye now.

And I'm out. Again.
Jubilant at the lie but hollow from the welcome.

She's right like. Imagine me in Paris. I am *part of the furniture*.
Veronica says that doesn't have to be a bad thing if I don't want
it to be and that Olivia is a patronising fuck.
I lost my mam in Wilton Shopping Centre when I was five and
I stood in the middle of the marbley floor screaming blue
murder. And when she didn't come, I climbed up on a plastic
giraffe ride that you put fifty pee into to make it go. I balanced
on the giraffe so I was more visible and I howled and wailed 'til
I popped all the blood vessels in my cheeks and a security man
grabbed me and did an announcement. That was the last time
I was lost.
You can't get lost in Cork.
I'd be constantly lost in Paris and there'd be no giraffe to stand
on.

Veronica's House

VERONICA! Are you up? I got you a surprise.

I'd passed a St Vincent de Paul shop on the way back to the flat
and I saw a miniscule brown bit of fur. It was a little lump of
bear with a flat face and black eyes that are just stitches. He is
peculiar and I knew she'd love him.

Look Ron, he's ridiculous.
Into her room and she's asleep in her clothes from last night,
a Debbie Harry T-shirt and leather skirt, cropped hair and about
ninety-seven earrings. She looks great, even in this state.
Cheekbones, y'know?

Don't ask me to get you Lucozade 'til after I've a shower. I'm
revolting. I'll get you water and a Nurofen first.

Dizzy in the kitchen, I hold myself up, gushing water into two
Budweiser glasses, soaking me and diluting the blood on my
top. Water drowns the unwashed plates and glasses I let pile up
while she was away sick

And as I stand there
I know
for certain
that Veronica is dead.

I bring the water and headache tablets into her.
I hold her waxy hand lying useless on the mattress.
She has short nails and veins near the surface which I always
thought was attractive but there's nothing much moving through
them any more.

I move the packets of pills from under her, one tablet left and
a half-empty bottle of Cork Dry Gin.
I lost count of the amount of times she rescued me.
And now...
And her skin is almost purple.
And that's the end of Veronica

And as the Gards and the ambulance finally pull away and
before her terrifying mother arrives...

I kind of know that no matter how long I live I won't find another one of her.
A pure one-off like, as they say.

And

Em.

I stay on her duvet for twenty-four hours or so.
I drink the rest of the gin.
I sit in the empty bath with the curtain closed and hope her ghost joins me.
Nothing.
Obviously.
And.

I call Olivia's house from the landline, a few times in the night and on the seventh time she answers but the sound of her voice after so long flummoxes me and I'm frozen.

And I don't say anything. I just listen to her questioning and tutting until.

Brenda?
If that's you
Will you
Just for once and for all leave us
Alone.
Will you?
Do you hear me?

My friend Olivia... do you remember Ver–

But she's put the phone down.
Back to Sam and English things and fancy art and thinking everyone is a dope.

I look up at the painting of her.
But.
It's not there?

Where is it?

Oh Christ.
I took it dancing.

I wanted her close to us when we went out. God. I showed it to randomers and boasted about her.

Look at her isn't she divine! Look!

And then.

Later.

Oh God.

Blurry feeling of scrawling on the painting in black marker, borrowed from the bar I suppose.

Scrawled hate.
You better lock your doors. I'm watching you. Stupid bitch. Liar. Whore.

And now it's?
Where is it?

It's

.

.

It's
Under the Welcome mat on her front door.
Hand-delivered.

Threats on her naked body.

Can't go to get it.
Obviously.

So. That's.

Don't know what time it is.
Light and dark stream in and out one by one and cover Veronica's bears. I pack them all, but one, in a suitcase with her My Little Pony pillow and a letter for her mam.

I pick up the phone to call Olivia again but I don't dial.

I spot a Sharpie behind the phone book.
Thick black, smelly lovely ink.

I mark my hand with it.
And sniff, mark and sniff, deeper and deeper into my arm until
it can't go any darker.
And then I stick a pin in my skin; from a brooch of a St Bridget's
cross that is on a calendar that was here when we moved in.
St Bridget is one of Ireland's patron saints y'know, very
important and she was… kind to everyone. And she used sleep
next to a younger woman in her bed and when Bridget died,
your one died exactly a year after her, which is, you know.

And I dig the cross into the top of my hand and follow it up
with ink from the pen time and time again. Pen and pin. Pen and
Pin. 'Til there's blood and Sharpie ink deep in me.
It's messy but you can read her name.
So I know it'll be there 'til I can afford to get it done properly.
Prison loyalty.
So she knows I will never stop thinking about her, no matter
what anyone says. She is the best person I'll ever meet.

I stare into the mirror at it, backwards but fantastic.
I think she'd like it.

Veronica.

Eight letters of fucking defiance.

Brian Boru Bridge. The Next Day

The sound of Veronica's mam howling is in my skull as the bus
pulls in.

The small flat bear I got for Veronica is at the top of my
handbag, watching the world go by. Everything else in a fat
mound in a backpack digging into my shoulders.

Overnight to Paris.

I hear him from the bridge and I fly to make it in time.
My heart is thumping, my face is flaming and my eyes
streaming from wind.

And I can hear Veronica saying:

That's it girl, go for it. This place is stultifying. Fly free like!
Just… if you don't go for any reason, will ya pick me up a
packet of Marlboro lights on your way back?

Unlooping the knots in my stomach at the thought of her and half-skidding, half-falling down the street, I make the bus.

And when I get there… To Paris.

Maybe I'll get a job in a café. Or a pastry shop.
And I'll put a bunch of daisies down for Veronica in the famous graveyard where Edith Piaf and Oscar Wilde are buried.
And I'll live a shiny shiny life for the both of us.

And after a few weeks, maybe five…

I'll call her, when I'm sure she's alone and I'll say
Olivia, I live in Paris now and I work with pastry and I am a size eight and I am writing a book about women and our hearts and lives and I am very centred and very very thin and I have the skin of an infant.

Maybe you could come and see me. I'm not desperate for you to but…
Maybe, nonetheless you could pop over to Paris and we could have a wander and just… see.

And she will arrive and and she will see me in floaty rose-coloured trousers and a little vintage top that says 'Nice Girls Do'.

And we will…
Hold hands… and…
Maybe

Just…

Just. Be. Together… again
There

Will we?
Maybe.

Or
Not…

Maybe
Not.

Maybe Not.

THE HALF OF IT

For Gabriel

The Half Of It was produced by MOMMO Theatre and first performed on 12 September 2017 as part of the Dublin Fringe Festival, with the following cast:

WOMAN	Karen Cogan
LINDA (*voice-over*)	Faoileann Cunningham

Director	Cathal Cleary
Designer	Kate Moylan
Lighting Designer	Bill Woodland
Sound Designer	Davy Kehoe
Costume Designer	Saileóg O'Halloran
Producer	Kelly Phelan

Characters

WOMAN
LINDA (*voice-over*)

Note on Text

The performer should be unafraid to differentiate between the
many people that appear in italics throughout.

Linda should be clearly distinct from Woman.

The space between text is indicative of the space around the
sections of speech.

Woman is without self-pity.

(*A bedsit in London. Maybe there are fresh stains on the carpet.*)

(*A* WOMAN *wakes up. She is crumpled and unable for life. 12.11 p.m. She has slept for as long as she can.*
She stands in her space. She turns the radio on. Static rings out. The radio springs to life and 'Knock Three Times' by Dawn plays.
She is transfixed by the sudden music. Perhaps she sways tensely.
The house does not smell good. She does not smell good. She walks to the window. She stands in front of it but makes no move to open it. This window will not be opened today. She stares out, into space.)

Woman
Woman
Man
Bus Stop
Smoking
Phone
Hello
Maggots
Stop
Mick Café
Morning Mick
Sandwich Board
Mick
Woman
Downturned mouth
Looks Irish or maybe Bulgarian
Woman
Girl
Dopey bitch
Stop

Mick Café
Stop
Stop
[This is] Pointless.

(*She gives up on the window.*)

(*She goes to a packet of biscuits and begins to eat. She chews some, well, and then spits out.*)

(*She sprays air freshener all over the space; and then, herself.*)

Putrid

No point crying over... No
It is a known fact that a life needs witnesses
Ssh!
If a tree falls in a forest and...
But shur...

Girl
No
Girl
NO
Mick Café
Boy
Boy
Brown
Lovely
Rushing
Stooped over
Can of

(*She stares.*)

Can of
Lager
Tanora
Energy drink
Green slash on the tin
Energy

For the day
Energy Boy

Three times more men kill themselves than women
Girls
Women
Ladies
Women
Three times more
Or two times
Suicide
Energy Boy is suicidal
He is
Killing himself because of
Not enough. Energy?
Too much energy?

Maybe his girlfriend died
Or his mother
Or his
Sister
Maybe his sister died and the boy can't cope at all
Maybe she
Lingered in a
Hospital 'til she died a bit
And then died completely
Or was knocked down by a speeding bike
Or got an infection and her blood turned septic and she died of
pus and poison
Or slit wrists sideways up the arms
Or murdered with a hammer after a rape
Or died when a baby was coming out of her
Or brain cancer
Or died on the operating –
Or fell and cracked her skull
Or
Or
Or
Okay
I hope someone put face cream on her. Before her coffin

Energy Boy doesn't seem very interested in creams. Maybe it
doesn't matter
No!
Good to keep up standards
Even when you're dead
Oil of Olay or

Stop

They jump off a bridge

The boys
Up to the top and
Off
Into the air
Must feel like – (*Carefully imagines the sensation of falling.*)
Whoooooooooooosh

Traffic though

What if
What if you land on a girl who just passed her driving test

Illegal to kill yourself
How can they punish you?

Why don't the girls kill themselves too?
Would you?
No

Why only the boys?
Mainly the boys?
How come?

Willies
Tough out
Man up
Hard as nails
Very brave
Man's man
Girls not brave
Girls crying
Ladies
Women

Weeping
And
Holding hands

Are they?
We weren't holding hands
We did not hold hands
You were not interested in my hand
Were you?

Except for one time
Once only
Adults
London town
Tight hands
Sweaty yours
And not-so-sweaty mine
But delighted to have some of your sweat
I wanted to go in there for you
Wanted to lay down on the black table thing and do it for you
But mostly
Most of all I wanted you to keep holding my hand
For months and months
Until
Tiny
Item
entered
Stop
No tiny item
Ssh
Only an operation
Or a
A procedure instead
Stop

Dirty hands
How often should you scrub your nails?
Always filthy

I only ever had two hands inside me
Number One

David Campion
Long yellow fingernails and he was always at himself wasn't he?
He put his thumb up me
Down an alley
Felt scratchy and huge
No thanks David
Let him put the thing itself inside of me instead so as not to
have to feel the thumb any more
Thumb felt more intimate than the real yoke
The peeen is
Fast and dry and done
Peee nis
Stupid word
What was Jamie Murphy's penis like?
Married penis
Maybe his wife chopped it off after ye did it
Up the
Vagina

Ears hot
Why?
Hot ears
The Smell making my ears hot?
Smells like
Eggs and rot
Rotty ears?
No
Ears burning
Hot ears
Ears burning
Means
Someone's talking about you
None of their business
Absolutely no need to talk about other people's business

Leave me to it
Leave me to be
What business is it of yours?
Keep your nose out of people's business
Don't be telling them my business
Under any circumstances

Why did you have to tell everyone everything?
Talking
What did you tell people about me
What did you say?
Hmm?
None of their

Dumpy
Weird
Quiet
Private business
About my life and
Our private business
Not on

Should have said nothing
Should have been trustworthy
Held my confidence
Held your tongue instead of
Should have been we
Whispery sisters instead of
Strangers
But

Foggy rainy day, us on the bed
You hungover
Me delighted you were staying in with me
For once
Remember episode three where she has the talk with that old
woman who puts drugs into her coffee
Straight in
To make her day better 'cause she'd no one
Where did she get the drugs?
Do you remember and our girl was wearing a beautiful dress

but she got soaked in the rain which was a shame but she didn't
mind 'cause it made her realise that everything was going to be
okay
Even when it was raining
And we had Maltesers and popcorn
The two of us
Sitting in a blanket
And you were laughing and you gave me your pyjama pants
'cause it was freezing
You had not topped up the gas card
That's why it was freezing
But
They were your favourite pyjama pants
Fleecy and with yellow polka dots
Made me feel like a bear or a toddler
Safe
And we watched eight episodes in a row
All through the night
Laughing and passing remarks
Shovel hands of popcorn and you made more and more 'til the
whole place stank of it
And it was
Safe and melty and
Then

Normal service resumed
Where are you going?
Dunno
Could you get the shopping?
Not today no
Are you coming back soon?
Yeah later
Later late?
Jesus back off
Gone
Door slammed
Nag
Left behind
All of a long Sunday

Sundays are endless
Sundays are a bad day
Sundays are cold
Sundays are like a big shop where there is a leak of yellow
water coming out of the wall and you don't know what you
went in for and your legs are mad itching and you stamp them
into the ground 'til wee comes out of you and everyone stares
and you drop the bottle of beer you're trying to pay for and it
smashes and cuts your hand and you bleed a lot of blood down
onto the wee and they hate you and they tell you to get out for
the way you speak at the checkout girl but she is patronising
and blotchy and confusing and
Stop

(There is noise from upstairs, heavy footsteps.
She freezes dead in her tracks.
She watches the ceiling.)

What did you say to Mam about me?
Hmm?
Ha?
Phone home
Hi Mam
Hiya

Standing
On her own
Flat
Call centre
Dry skin
No friends
Will not go to the bar
Will not drink a Campari and talk to the men
Has not changed
Is the same
Not cut out for London
Very weird
Very peculiar girl
Dopey bitch God forgive me
More in her line to come home

Isn't it
Better suited to her to be home
Easier
Simpler for her
London is very
Fish out of
Loopy
She's after getting very big
In very bad form
Mean
Itchy
Obsessed
Very hard oover
For her
Locked door
No sign of her doing anything
Lists on the wall
In marker
Controlling maybe
Who draws on a good wall
Weirdo

Call centre
Home
Call centre
Home
Call centre
Home
Call centre
Home
Hello I'm calling from
I see that you have supported us in the past
Hello I'm calling from
I see you
Hello
I see that you've supported us
(*English.*) *Can you remove me please*
Stop ringing me
Don't ring
Stop ringing us

Is there no other job you could get my love?
Stop fucking ringing me or I swear to God
I swear to God You stop ringing me
What? I'm not. You rang me
You stop ringing me
Stop it

Is that what you told them Linda?
Pathetic
Me
And successful
You
You are fancy and chatty and good
And I am rotting and peculiar

You are glamour and shiny bar stools and people in and out of
the flat
No people in the flat Linda! I told you. Our flat.
That's that
But then you didn't come home for two full weeks did ya and
I couldn't bear you not being here
Me
Wandering and doing
Nothing
My own face in the window and the mirror and the screen
Watching out the window
Mick Café
Strangers passing
Boy
Woman
Phone
And just me
Me
So when you finally walked in
'Okay. People welcome in the flat. People in the flat no
problem.'
And then a steady stream of them
Even though you were actually
Filthy
Tampons in the toilet

Blood clogging
Left there no matter how many times
No shame
I scrambled to hide the dirt and the pubes of you
From your friends so they couldn't see the grubbiness
And you
Free
Friends
And dancing
Dancing in tops
Put on some music and just
C'mon dance
Me still
Stupefied
Dance for God's sake
Dance
Dance Girl
Dance C'mon Dance Dance with me Dance c'mon Dance
DANCE

You look so fucking ugly Linda do you know that.
Disgrace
In front of them

And I pulled the radio out of the wall and punched in the
speakers with my fingers
So I didn't have to look at you
Gyrating
Weird
Private
Didn't want to be looking at you doing that
So I smashed it
There
Easy to break
Cheap
Came with the flat
Long gone

But you wouldn't let up
You wouldn't settle
Why couldn't we just settle in?

Just us two
That's all I
Not so much to ask in return
Nothing else
You and me
Staying here
Safe
And telly
Warm telly
And lovely
But no
Let's go here
Let's go out
Why aren't you in work today
What's wrong with you
Perfume
And your belly button poking out of tops
Feelings and friends
Strangers
In our place
Pads and knickers and
Always looking for something better
Settle

Let's try a class
Let's go and look at a thing
Come to the pub one time
Come on we go out
Why don't you meet me here
Let's learn a thing
Let's invite them over
Let's run
Let's do a course
Let's get pissed
Let's knit a blanket
Let's make and dance and move and invite weirdos into the flat
and tell new people things about us that are none of their
fucking business and prance around and talk with a ridiculous
English accent even though we had only been here a small
while are we're IRISH

Was here not nice enough?
Little flat
Me
I bought Sweet Williams for the window
Keep it nice
Always
In case
Lit a tealight
But you never saw it
Eight hours burning guaranteed

Gallivanting as they say
Gallivanting
What did you tell them?

Linda?
What did you say?
Linda?

(*The phone rings. She is utterly cowed by the noise.
It rings out to silence.*)

Awful
Interruption
No

No need for constant
Noise
People have no peace

(*Noise from upstairs.
She is consumed by a feeling at the noise but paralysed to take
action.*)

(*She finds the fleecy pyjama pants with the yellow polka dots
and puts them on.*)

Now
Lovely

And now what?

Now what?

Hmm?

Go

Outside?

Like this?
In your

Go outside
Yes
The big door
The door downstairs
Twenty-seven steps
And
Big door
Front door
Door and then
Air
In my face
And
What?
Outside

And
See
Who?

Strangers
No

Just
Outside

But first
The door
The door
The door
The door
The door
The door
The door
Stop

No door
Just

Bridge
Suicide Bridge
Danger
Off the bridge and
Whooosh
Be cold on my skin
I think
Refreshing
Air
Air
To breathe
for a minute
Fast air before
Blood on the pyjamas
Lots
You'd be fuming
No

Bridge is a twenty-minute walk away
Twenty minutes
Twenty
And with spikes on the top
To stop the pigeons
Or
I don't know
Pigeons aren't jumping off bridges
There's no need for them to jump
They can
Fly
Obviously
No sense

So the bars are for people so
So how many people have jumped off it?
How hard is to get on top of it
How do you get there if not in a car?
Do my legs go twenty minutes?

Thousands of steps
Stop
But
What if you land in front of an old man whose brother just got
diagnosed with cancer
Or a baby in a car seat?
What if a toddler sees you
Dead and twisted after the fall
What if you really upset a stray dog

Remember when that student threw himself off the College of
Commerce
Or
The Shaky Bridge
Penneys
Off of Mam's house
Off in front of the number 5 bus to The Lough
Imagine if you jumped in front of Uncle Jonny
Does Uncle Jonny even still drive the buses?
Jesus Mary Mother of God
Is that your one after jumping in front of the bus
Dopey bitch God forgive me
What in the name of God is she at
In that top
Like a whore
She's not married at all y'know
Single still
Dead now anyway
So neither here nor there now
Ah, still though

I hope someone puts face cream on me
If the box is open?
Maybe closed so as to hide the
No

She looks great anyway
Very herself
Isn't it?
I was just saying there Moira, doesn't she look beauutiful?

She does
Doesn't she?
She could almost be
She could
But she's not
Is she?

Are you on your way back here?
Linda?
'Cause
I could
I could live in the cupboard maybe
And you could have the flat
I'd be starved though
No
But
They did used to bury women inside buildings
And bridges
As a punishment for whatever thing they did wrong
They'd put them into a little hole with a bit of food and then
just build walls around them 'til there was no escape and leave
them to die.
They might bring them water so they would stay alive longer
and sometimes they stayed alive for years.

Would you bring me a sandwich or

No

(*She stares at the ceiling.*)

Did she stay with you overnight?
I know that you were mad about her
Mad about her

Up and down the stairs to her day and night
Lovely to hear ye both stomping through the floors 'til three
o'clock in the morning
Not fair
Stomping
Selfish

Cruel behaviour on me
And
And
Sex noises
Sex noise
Sex noises

Disgusting

She's
And she smells of oil and her hands are
Rough
And you couldn't get enough of her
Up
Down
Thud thud stomp stomp day and night
You just threw your bag in the door and not even a hello

Linda?
Did you do the list?
Did you finish the list?
Did you get the shopping?
I need something
Did you pay the electricity?
Linda?
Did you get what I asked you to get?
Linda ?
Linda???

Nothing
No basic
Not enough help
Just me
Day and day and day and day and day and day and no you

I said you could have people here
Against my will
But no
Not good enough for you
Instead the noise
Over and over
Racket

Constant
Bad enough when just her up there but now you
My sister
Up there ruining my days
And I couldn't
Bear it
The bed
The bed and your voice
Strangled and sex
And her
On top of you
And why can't you just come down here
To me
Stay here with me

(*She screams at the ceiling, almost wild.*)

JUST
GET DOWN HERE LINDA

(*Pause.*)

I came over with you
I gave you my hand when you were scared
Mawkish skinny English nurse cocking her head to the side and
I did the papers for you and I helped you and I paid for it.
Every penny from the video shop.
Got a fat boy fired because they thought he was squirrelling
away the euros but instead it was me

I told Mam
Linda has an interview
Big interview and I'm going to move over with her
Well, I'll just quit for now. I can always come back to it
I know it's a good job but London
And Linda needs a flatmate
So it's better me than some stranger
You two are thick as thieves suddenly
We are ya
We are thick as thieves suddenly
Flatmates

London
New
Better me
Than some God-knows-what over
God knows who
So
Saving waiting booking
Until
Time!
No fuss
No one at the door to wave goodbye
Couldn't get out fast enough
Plane
Squished in
Couldn't talk about what was about to happen 'cause of all the
people nearby
Breaking the law
Thelma and Louise
Not really
No word from you
I gave you a sandwich
Shaking hand
Sick stomach you said
Morning sickness my hole
Gawking balls of vomit in the airport toilet and once on the tray
table
Peculiar dry vomit sticking to your face
Disaster
But I had you

In the clinic
Linda
Are you sure?
Are you sure?
Because I could?
Mind it
And what harm?
I might sing it a song and take it to the to the
To the

West End and
The and the
Tate
And it would be such a fancy life
London baby
And imagine that
The two of us
A small family

Disgusted
Disgusted at the notion
I'm not ready
It was a mistake
I'm not able for this
So
Stop
My choice
Nothing to do with you
My body
Stop It now love
Please

Let go of my hand and let the English people take it out of you

It would have been
No

A
walnut
Then a bigger nut
Then a fruit
Then a bigger fruit
Then a pineapple
A pineapple
And soon
A baby
No

Quiet
Couldn't say anything to you
About babies

So
I drew pictures
And wrote a story in a book
Secret
Secret stories and planning for us three even though no one else
was coming

You were shaky and bloody and gentle at first
Soft and here
And grateful
For the help
Lovely
But then
Relieved
Better
Free
Healthy
Gone
Running off in jeans
Skinny as anything
Pulling pints
Cash under the table
New life for Linda
New lease of

Door slam
Gone
Door
Gone
So
Notebook
Yes
Keeping track in my book and writing down things
About the call centre
And about me
Your mam used get bullied badly by Anita Cummins but I
slapped Anita from below and got her in the nose and it pumped
blood all down her school uniform and she never bothered us
again. Thick as thieves.

And it would have liked me
And we could have stayed in and watched things

I could have shown it *Beaches*. All about two girls who have the
summer to end all summers…
Even if you weren't ready
I might have been
Babies just eat and sleep and want to watch telly and
Stay in
Maybe

But that's
Weird
Not my choice
Apparently
Not on
You could have just got pregnant a different time couldn't you?

(*Sings.*) It must have been cold there in my shadow
Stop

Locked door
Door slam
Nothing
Barren maybe
Never know
Neither here nor there anyway

Together
Imagine
Imagine?
Us two
Mams
You'd rather die

We should have gone to Syria.
What would we have done though

I was sorry to hear. Sorry for your misfortune
I apologise to hear about your accident
No
Get well

You're gone
But you don't live here any more I think so
So
Me
No one

You should come back

I can't get out
And now
How will I
Linda?
How will I

Sure
But sure look
Lookit
Anyway
But shur
Ah you're as well off
We're all grand
You'll be better before you're married
What doesn't kill you makes you
Well
God only gives us what we can handle
It is the strong man who
Not a man though
Girl
Lady
Woman

Stop

You used to be there.
Didn't you?
Do you remember?
No
All gone

Anyway

Will we watch telly?

Can you just occasionally flush the toilet after yourself no?
Poo particles in the air.

John shat three times today in four hours
That's a new record
Even for him
Plops through the wall
Smells of cock and lavender leaking in
You look tired
Was the bar mental
Were the fellas all over you?
Are you coming home after your shift?
Okay
I'm only asking

Did you bring the teabags?

Jesus fucking Christ Linda
Why can't you just bring the teabags
It's on the wall in permanent marker
I can't make it any bigger
Barry's Tea Bags before they run out
Chops for Tuesday
Chicken on Wednesday with roast potatoes in a bag
Peas and sweetcorn and ham on Thursday
Chips on Friday with
And
You're never here on Saturday
Sunday
So
Why is it so hard
I just want things nice
Normal
Simple
Why can't you just settle?

I put your shoes in the bin
Red trainers

Binned
But didn't stop you
No stopping you
Where are you going?
Where are you going?

If you go up there to her again
I will not be responsible
You lesbian
You dirty
Stinking
Sorry
But
I can hear you
I can hear ye
Do you understand
Through the night
And
And thudding
And

(She makes sex noises and bangs.
She is driven demented by the memory.)

Yes I went up to her
Linda
No chops
No tea bags
No simple respect
No love
No basic
No interest
In me
Whatsoever

Knock on her door knock
Knock
Yes knock
Yes I made a friend
Like you wanted
Socialising isn't that what you wanted me to do?

Hello
No Linda's fine
She's not in
I just wanted to
Can I?
And there she was
All round and soft and kinda friendly and kind of confused
But she had wine
Two for a fiver from downstairs
White
Vinegar
But down the hatch
And put my finger on her breastbone
Here
Then another finger and another
And lower
Her skin was freckly and I hated her
But I touched her
And she said *No no*
Linda would be very

I said that you were kissing loads of people
Boys and girls
In our flat
Very casual
Not true
Not true at all
You
Dreamed about her and said her name at four in the morning

Linda is actually quite serious with a man named
Graham
Upset face
Tear
Another tear
Cross
But more sour wine
Kept pouring and
Touching arms
And watching a programme about animals

Buffalo
Until she's bleary
And I put a kiss on her
And she puts one back
Half-hearted
But
And I hold her horrible chest
And let her do the finger things that ye were doing
And I hear you come home downstairs

And I got very loud and I got very very loud upstairs
So you would know
And I pounded myself into the floor
So you could hear
And I writhed and screamed and pretended
Felt mad
Felt wild

When I just wanted very badly to be with you in the flat in your
warm pyjamas with tea and a TV show after having the right
dinner at the right time
With you

With you
Didn't we move over to be together
Didn't we?
Or was I just until you didn't need a sister any more
Me on my own while you flit around
London Linda
Fits right in
Sexy
Gyrating
Selfish
Stupid

Back down
To face your face

Steaming
Red

Streaming tears all
Pooling in your

I can't believe she would touch you
She wouldn't. You must have forced her

I didn't need to force her

Didn't admit to my lie
Graham

What's wrong with you? Seriously though
Why is your face so crooked?
Your nose jutting out
Everyone laughs at you. They wait for stories about you at the
bar
I tell them everything about you.
How you lock yourself in the flat and never walk outside
Ever
How you won't shit in your own home 'til everyone in the
building is at work
How you went ten days without a shit because you were so
petrified someone would hear the plop
How you bleed through your ratty tracksuit pants every single
month even though you got your first period when you were nine
and should have it sorted after two fucking decades
How you used to run home from your zero-hours job and pelt in
the door and triple lock it even at 4 p.m. in June
Before you even lost that
Hermit
Petrified
Useless
What is the point?
You hate everyone and trust no one and how you are fucking
obsessed with me
Obsessed
You fill notebooks with made-up stories for a thing that never
even existed
Never even close
Jesus Christ

Do you want to marry me? Do you want that? Married lunatic
sisters penned behind a locked door for the rest of our lives?
Ha?
Fucking psycho

I shouldn't have
Pushed
You
Didn't think my arms would let me
But
Won't get over the sight
Shattered your bone
Collarbone
When you fell
So peculiar to see it poking out through your chest
If you hadn't hit the coffee table maybe we would have been
Grand
Her calling the ambulance
You screaming blue murder
Threw up on the carpet
Shattered
Poking bone
Open doors
All of them
Wind blowing up the stairs
And then a
Man
Shouting questions
Who's coming in the ambulance?

Not her
Don't let her – Do you hear me? Do you hear me?
I hear you
Blue lights
Clattering trolley
Gone

No more sister
Empty

And
Now what?

Now what

What?
What will you do?
Police
Her
Stories about me
Court
Outside
Door
What

Door got very heavy
While ago
Years ago
Couldn't seem to get outside
Like you could
You zipped out
I tried to push the big doors but my stomach
Tried to go out and
Tried
But out was impossible
It is impossible
It's a very heavy door
By anyone's standards
And couldn't bear to see
People
To face
Strangers

And now
The
Thing I did
To your heart
And your bones
Your bone

So just

Don't go
Don't bring grapes
No Lucozade
Don't say sorry
Don't show up
Don't hold your hand
This time

So
Me
Me
Gone you
Me
Hiding
Standing
Sitting
Doing nothing
Locked door
Phone
Nothing
Listening
For her
In case she
Knocks
Or
Someone comes and

So

I'm
Sorry
I'm sorry I'm really sorry okay? I'm sorry I'm saying sorry I
said sorry I'm sorry sorry I'm very sorry okay? Sorry I'm sorry
I'm saying sorry I'm sorry okay? Sorry like Sorry I said sorry
Sorry I'm sorry like
Sorry?

Better before you're married
What doesn't kill you makes you

What if you fall in front of two sisters going out to celebrate
their exam results
Sisters
In tops and going
Dancing

That'd be
Unfair

(*She faces herself in a mirror and puts on face cream.*)

But shur look

(*She faces the door and, without putting on shoes or coat, and,
with difficulty, she walks outside.*)

(*As the door closes behind her and she is gone, the phone rings.
And rings.*)

(*It rings out and goes to a beep.*)

(*Linda's voice, Cork, young, fills the flat.*)

LINDA (*voice-over.*) Hello?

Hello?
Answer the phone
Answer the fucking phone

Are you for real?
Are you actually not coming? I'm here on my own like

I should get the police on to you
But…

I've said it was an accident
That you weren't very well in yourself and you didn't mean to
cause any… damage
I can't believe this
I know you're not quite…
I know it's hard

It really hurts… And no one is visiting
And, the woman next to me is dying and everyone is bawling
And her daughters are constantly here and

Could you come?
Please?
Come down to me?

Could you bring me my spotty pyjamas and a pillow. And
maybe a Wispa. The food is shite

Please
I'm in the main women's ward. Take the 68 down and get off at
the hospital and straight in? It's close by. Please
Okay love? Okay?

Hello?

(*The voicemail beeps off and the lights snap to dark.*)

(*End.*)

A Nick Hern Book

Drip Feed and The Half Of It first published in Great Britain in 2018 as a paperback original by Nick Hern Books Limited, The Glasshouse, 49a Goldhawk Road, London W12 8QP, in association with Soho Theatre

Drip Feed and The Half Of It copyright © 2018 Karen Cogan

Karen Cogan has asserted her moral right to be identified as the author of these works

Cover photograph by Gabriel Pac

Designed and typeset by Nick Hern Books, London
Printed in the UK by Mimeo Ltd, Huntingdon, Cambridgeshire PE29 6XX

A CIP catalogue record for this book is available from the British Library

ISBN 978 1 84842 785 3

www.nickhernbooks.co.uk

facebook.com/nickhernbooks

twitter.com/nickhernbooks